For My Grandchild

For My Grandchild

A Grandmother's Gift
of Memory

Sterling Publishing Co., Inc.
New York

Created and produced by Lark Books

Text: Paige Gilchrist

Design: Kristi Pfeffer

AARP Books include a wide range of titles on health, personal finance, lifestyle, and other subjects to enrich the lives of 50+ Americans.

For more information, go to www.aarp.org/books

AARP, established in 1958, is a nonprofit, nonpartisan organization with more than 35 million members age 50 and older. The views expressed herein do not necessarily represent the policies of AARP and should not be construed as endorsements.

The AARP name and logo are registered trademarks of AARP, used under license to Sterling Publishing Co., Inc.

10 9 8 7 6 5 4 3 2

Published by Sterling Publishing Co., Inc.
387 Park Avenue South, New York, N.Y. 10016

© 2005 by Sterling Publishing Co., Inc.

Distributed in Canada by Sterling Publishing
c/o Canadian Manda Group, 165 Dufferin Street
Toronto, Ontario, Canada M6K 3H6
Distributed in Great Britain by Chrysalis Books Group PLC
The Chrysalis Building, Bramley Road, London W10 6SP, England
Distributed in Australia by Capricorn Link (Australia) Pty. Ltd.
P.O. Box 704, Windsor, NSW 2756, Australia

Manufactured in China

Sterling ISBN 13: 978-1-4027-2325-4
       ISBN 10: 1-4027-2325-3

For information about custom editions, special sales, premium and corporate purchases, please contact Sterling Special Sales Department at 800-805-5489 or specialsales@sterlingpub.com.

Contents

A Note to Grandmother

Grandmothers these days are different. In addition to doting on their grandchildren, they're working at full- or part-time jobs, traveling around foreign countries, running (or running in) political campaigns, taking classes, and embarking on second careers as everything from artists to investors.

But as full and active as life is for you and other grandmothers today, two things haven't changed. Like generations of grandmothers before you, you still think the little person your son or daughter has brought into your life is one of the most precious beings in the universe. And you are still one of the strongest and most special links your grandchild has to the family history, heritage, and traditions that will help shape who he or she will grow to be. Sooner or later, your grandchild is going to want to know everything about that history and heritage—and, especially, about you and your story. This book is for the telling.

For My Grandchild lets you carry on a personal conversation with your grandchild, recording written and visual details as you go. You're guided easily through the process of reliving the past and reflecting on who you are today by helpful, fun-to-answer questions, voiced from the perspective of a curious grandchild. There are straightforward fill-in-the-blanks for specifics such as family-tree information and the details of your wedding day. And there are broader questions that give you room to riff on everything from the fashions, hairstyles, and hangouts that were popular when you were a teenager to the people who influenced you early on and the principles that guide you today.

Because contemporary grandmothers are a diverse lot, this book allows ample opportunity for every grandmother to personalize her approach and make it truly her own. Many of the general questions come with prompts to help you get started. *(Tell me about college. What was your major? Were you in a sorority or did you work on the school newspaper?)* You can respond to them directly or toss out the prompts and even the question, and use the space to write about what you did instead, such as flee to the nearest big city right after high school, eager to live on your own, or spend a year traveling with the band.

Make the book your own visually, too. It's filled with space for pasting photos, with graphic backgrounds designed to frame images of all sizes, shapes, and orientations. One page might hold your favorite black-and-white photo of your grandparents; another can be a lively collage of family holiday snapshots and handwritten captions. Interspersing clippings, concert tickets, quotes, copies of letters, and so on works too. More pages in the back give you extra space for mementos and memorabilia.

No matter how much has changed, as a grandmother today, you're still the natural chronicler of your family's story, the bridge between the past and the future. Chances are, you'll enjoy the process of piecing together that story—and telling about the special roles you and your grandchild play in it—as much as grandmothers have throughout time. Now you have a way to capture and preserve all the story's details as a keepsake book for generations to come.

Put a photo of
yourself here

Tell Me
About You

Your name (first, middle, maiden, married)

Were you named after anyone?

Do you have any nicknames? How did you get them?

I call you _____. Where does that name come from?

Who are you besides my grandmother?
Gardener, businessperson, traveler, committee member, hiker?

Your Current Favorites

_____
Books (or other things to read)

_____
Music

_____
Vacation spot

_____
Way to spend time with friends

_____
Way to goof off

_____
Way to stay fit

_____
Movies or TV shows

_____
Foods

_____
Thing to collect

_____
Political, religious, or social cause

_____
Part about being the age you are now

Why did you decide to create this book for me?

_____
_____
_____
_____
_____
_____
_____
_____
_____
_____
_____
_____
_____
_____
_____
_____
_____
_____
_____
_____

PHOTO PAGE
Put a photo of you
and your grandchild
on this page

me

_____
Name

_____
Birth date

_____
Place of birth

_____
Name

_____
Birth date

_____
Place of birth

_____
Name

_____
Birth date

_____
Place of birth

my parents

grandmother

_____
Name

_____
Birth date

_____
Place of birth

_____
Name

_____
Birth date

_____
Place of birth

grandfather

_____
Name

_____
Birth date

_____
Place of birth

_____
Name

_____
Birth date

_____
Place of birth

great-grandparents

_____
Name

_____
Birth date

_____
Place of birth

_____
Name

_____
Birth date

_____
Place of birth

_____
Name

_____
Birth date

_____
Place of birth

_____
Name

_____
Birth date

_____
Place of birth

great-great-grandparents

What's my heritage?

Where are my ancestors from? When did they come to this country, and why?
Where did they settle and what did they do there?

_____

_____

_____

_____

_____

_____

_____

_____

_____

_____

Tell me about your mom and dad (my great-grandparents).

Where did they grow up? When did they get married? How did they earn their living? What's something
you'd like me to know about your mom? About your dad? What are some of the most important
things you learned from your parents?

_____

_____

_____

_____

_____

_____

_____

_____

_____

PHOTO PAGE
Put a photo or photos
of your parents on this page,
and add captions if you like

Tell me about your grandparents (my great-great-grandparents).

When were they married? What did they do for a living, and how many kids did they have?
What do you remember most about them?

On your mom's side:

On your dad's side:

PHOTO PAGE

Put photos of your
grandparents on this page, and
add captions if you like

What about your brothers and sisters (my great-aunts and great-uncles)?

How did you all get along when you were growing up? What did you do together for fun? What's the most trouble you ever got into together (and what happened when your parents found out)? If you were an only child, what was that like? Were there cousins or friends who were like siblings?

Name

Birth date

Place of birth

Name

Birth date

Place of birth

Name

Birth date

Place of birth

Name

Birth date

Place of birth

PHOTO PAGE
Put photos of your
siblings on this page,
and add captions if you like

PHOTO PAGE
Put a favorite family
photo or two on this page,
and add captions if you like

Tell me more about our family.

Who are some of our relatives everyone considers most successful? How about most interesting or eccentric?

Who are the best family storytellers, and what do they tell about?

Who am I most like, and why?

Is there anyone famous (or infamous) in our family?

When You Were a Little Girl

Where did you live?
Was it in a house, an apartment, on a farm? Did you move around a lot?

What was your family life like?
Were your parents strict? What were some household rules? What did your family do for vacations, trips, or other fun times together? Did you have family pets?

Tell me about school.

What subjects and activities did you like most in school? Which were your least favorite?
Were you shy or outgoing?

What about outside school?

Did you take any lessons, like piano or dance? What were your favorite toys, books, or comics?
When did your family get a television? What were your favorite shows?

What were some of your favorite holidays, and how did your family celebrate them?
Any special decorating traditions? What about traditional meals or foods? Did you have a favorite
Halloween costume?

Who's the first president you remember?

Any famous people (singers, movie stars) you had crushes on?

What did you daydream about being or doing when you grew up?

PHOTO PAGE
Put a photo or photos
of yourself when you were
little on this page, and
add captions if you like

When You Were a
Teenager & Young Woman

What were you like in high school?
What were your favorite subjects? What activities did you participate in (sports teams, cheerleading, French club, band)? Who was your favorite teacher and what made him or her so special?

What were the coolest fashions and hairstyles?
Which ones did you wear? Did your school have dress codes? Did you ever break them?

PHOTO PAGE
Put a photo or photos
of yourself as a teenager
on this page, and add
captions if you like

Tell me about your social life.
What were some of the most fun (or wildest) things you and your friends did? Did you have a curfew?

What about dating?
Where did you go on dates? Do you remember your first date? Did you have a steady boyfriend?

What were the
popular hangouts?

What kind of music did you listen to?

Who were your favorite singers or bands? How about favorite songs? Did you buy a lot of records?
Go to a lot of concerts? Spend hours listening to the radio? What were the popular dances?

Did you have a car?

What was it? How much did it cost? Who taught you how to drive, and how did that go?

Tell me about college.

Where did you go? What was your major? What activities (maybe a sorority or the newspaper) were you involved in? What were you like—studious, a hippie, the life of the party?

What was going on in the world?
Were you active in any social or political causes? Were there famous people—political leaders, activists, artists—who had a big influence on you?

Did you pursue a career after high school or college?
What were some of your earliest jobs? What were some of the most challenging things about being a woman in the work world when you entered it?

PHOTO PAGE

Put a photo or photos
of yourself as a young
woman on this page, and
add captions if you like

When You Married
My Grandfather

How did you meet my grandfather?

Where did you go on your first date? What were some of the best times
you had together when you were dating? What did you like most about him then?

How did he propose? (Or maybe you proposed to him?)

What did your parents say when you told them you were getting married? How long were you engaged?

All About Grandfather

_____
Name

_____
Parents

_____

_____

_____
Brothers and sisters

_____

_____
Where he grew up

_____
When he graduated from high school

_____

_____
What he did afterward

Your Wedding

_____

Date

_____

Time

_____

Place

_____

_____

What you wore

_____

_____

Flowers you carried

_____

_____

Songs that were played

_____

_____

_____

_____

The reception

PHOTO PAGE
Put one of your
wedding photos here,
and add a caption
if you like

Special memories of that day

The honeymoon

Becoming a
Mom

Tell me about when my parent was born.
When? Where? How did you and grandfather feel when your baby was born?

_____

_____

_____

_____

_____

What was my parent like as a small child? As a teenager?
What are some of my parent's talents and gifts that you noticed early on? What are some things my parent did in childhood or as a teenager that made you happy? How about some that drove you crazy? What did you think my parent might grow up to be?

Put a photo of
yourself as a
young mom here

What were some of the things you liked best about being a mom when my parent was a child? What were some of the toughest things?

PHOTO PAGE
Put a photo or photos
of you and your child
on this page, and
add captions if you like

How do I remind you of my parent?

How am I different?

What are some of the things that make you proud of my parent today?

When I Was Born

How did my parents tell you I was on the way?

What was your reaction?

When did you first meet me?
Do you remember how you felt when you held me for the first time? When you bragged about me afterward, what did you say? Did you think I resembled anyone in the family?

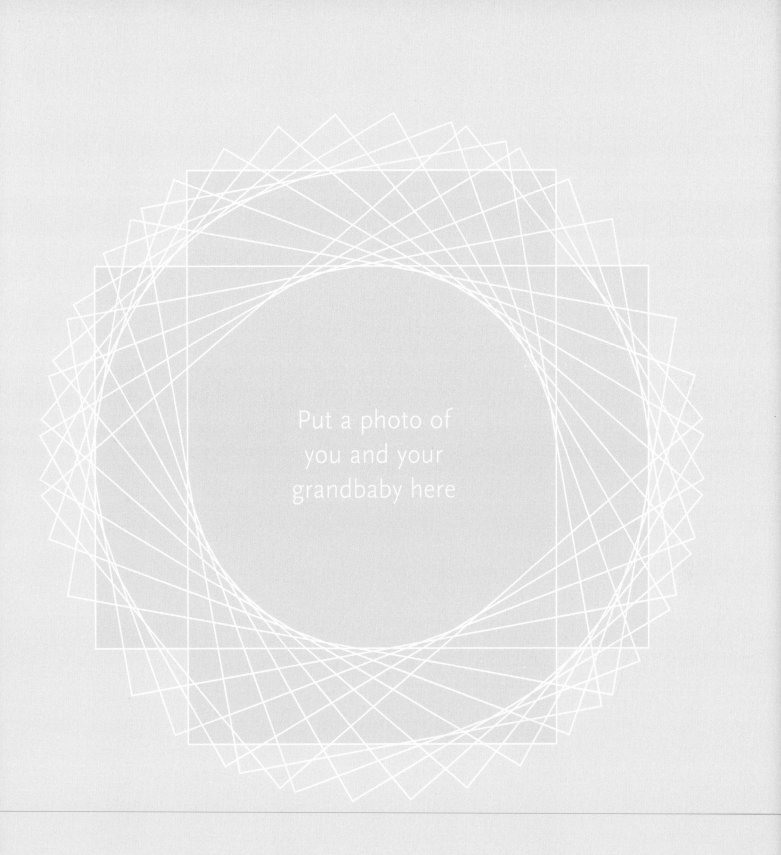

Put a photo of
you and your
grandbaby here

What do you like about being a grandmother?

Is there anything you don't like?

How has being a grandmother changed you?

PHOTO PAGE

Put a photo or photos
of you and your grandchild
on this page, and add
captions if you like

Holidays

Of all the holidays our family celebrates, which are your favorites, and where do our traditions come from?

_____

Are some of our traditions from when
you were a little girl or when
my parent was little?

_____

What family dishes do we
always serve?

What about special ways
we decorate?

First

Kiss

Pet

Trip somewhere on your own

Place you lived on your own

Presidential candidate you ever voted for

Photos • Mementos • Photos • Mementos

Favorite

Place you've ever lived

Fashion breakthoughs in your lifetime

Times spent with your children

Times spent with your grandchildren

Favorite

Places you've traveled to

_____

_____

_____

_____

_____

Jobs you've had

_____

_____

_____

_____

_____

Causes you've volunteered for

_____

_____

_____

_____

Quote

66

_____

_____

_____

99

Photos • Mementos • Photos • Mementos

Most Important

Political or religious leaders in your lifetime

_____

_____

Social movements in your lifetime

_____

_____

Inventions or discoveries that have made your life better or easier

Role models or mentors in your life

Sources of strength and support in your life

_____

_____

Piece of advice you want to pass on to me

_____

_____

_____

_____

Photos • Mementos • Photos • Mementos

Photos • Mementos • Photos • Mementos

Biggest

Adventure you've had

Adventure you'd still like to have

Risks you've taken

World event in your lifetime—one so important that you remember exactly where you were when you learned of it

Lessons you've learned

Accomplishment

Person Who

You looked up to most as a girl

You admire most now

You've learned the most from

Photos • Mementos • Photos • Mementos

Looking Back Now

The things you've found most important in life

The things people tend to make a big deal about that really aren't that important after all

Values you cherish

Principles that guide you

Words to live by

Experiences you hope I will have

Traditions you would most like to pass on to me

Never...

Always...

A Map of Your World

Tell me some of the memorable places you've lived, when you were there, and what you were doing, such as going to school, starting your first job, or raising your children.

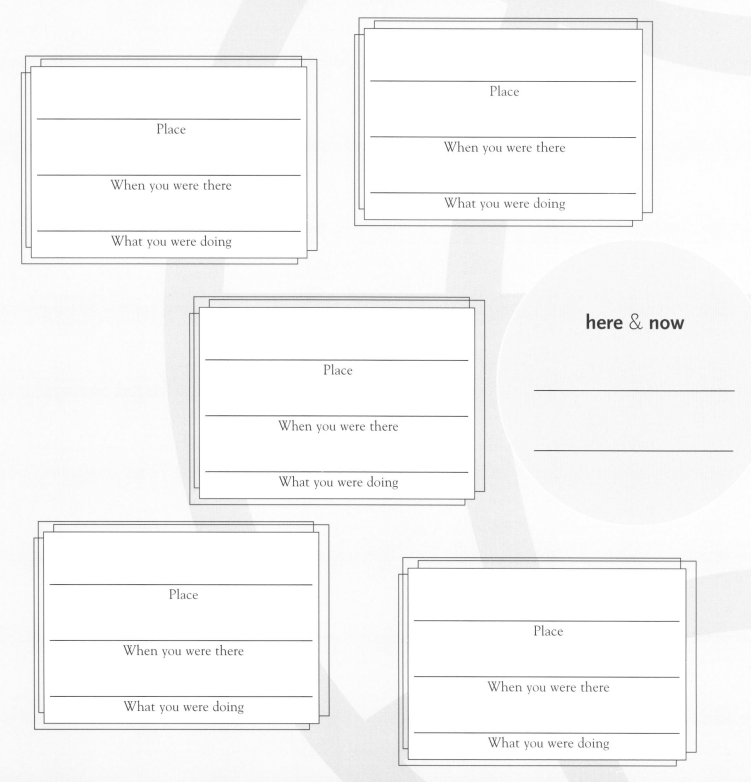

Place

When you were there

What you were doing

Place

When you were there

What you were doing

Place

When you were there

What you were doing

here & now

Place

When you were there

What you were doing

Place

When you were there

What you were doing

Place

When you were there

What you were doing

Place

When you were there

What you were doing

Place

When you were there

What you were doing

Place

When you were there

What you were doing

Place

When you were there

What you were doing

Place

When you were there

What you were doing

Place

When you were there

What you were doing

A Map of Your World

Fill these pages with photos of places you've lived, and add captions if you like.

Photos • Mementos • Photos • Mementos

Photos • Mementos • Photos • Mementos

Grandmother's
Favorite Recipes

Fill these pages with copies of favorite family
recipes you want to hand down to me.

More Memories

Add more photos and life treasures on the next few pages.

Photos • Mementos • Photos • Mementos

Photos • Mementos • Photos • Mementos

Photos • Mementos • Photos • Mementos

Photos • Mementos • Photos • Mementos